Acceptance
&
Gratitude

Look for these topics in the
Everyday Matters Bible Studies for Women

Acceptance	Mentoring
Bible Study & Meditation	Outreach
Celebration	Prayer
Community	Reconciliation
Confession	Sabbath & Rest
Contemplation	Service
Faith	Silence
Fasting	Simplicity
Forgiveness	Solitude
Gratitude	Stewardship
Hospitality	Submission
Justice	Worship

Acceptance
&
Gratitude

Spiritual Practices
FOR EVERYDAY LIFE

HENDRICKSON
PUBLISHERS

**Everyday Matters Bible Studies for Women—
Acceptance & Gratitude**

© 2014 by Hendrickson Publishers Marketing, LLC
P.O. Box 3473
Peabody, Massachusetts 01961-3473

ISBN 978-1-61970-147-2

Printed in the United States of America

Second Printing — June 2014

Contents

Gratitude

Holy Habits

Spiritual Practices for Everyday Life

Everyday life today is busier and more distracting than it has ever been before. While cell phones and texting make it easier to keep track of children and each other, they also make it harder to get away from the demands that overwhelm us. Time, it seems, is a shrinking commodity. But God, the Creator of time, has given us the keys to leading a life that may be challenging but not overwhelming. In fact, he offers us tools to do what seems impossible and come away refreshed and renewed. These tools are called spiritual practices, or spiritual disciplines.

Spiritual practices are holy habits. They are rooted in God's word, and they go back to creation itself. God has hardwired us to thrive when we obey him, even when it seems like his instructions defy our "common sense." When we engage in the holy habits that God has ordained, time takes on a new dimension. What seems impossible is actually easy; it's easy because we are tapping into God's resources.

The holy habits that we call spiritual practices are all geared to position us in a place where we can allow the Holy Spirit to work in us and through us, to grant us power and strength to do the things we can't do on our own. They take us to a place where we can become intimate with God.

While holy habits and everyday life may sound like opposites, they really aren't.

As you learn to incorporate spiritual practices into your life, you'll find that everyday life is easier. At the same time, you will draw closer to God and come to a place where you can luxuriate in his rich blessings. Here is a simple example. Elizabeth Collings hated running household errands. Picking up dry cleaning, doing the grocery shopping, and chauffeuring her kids felt like a never-ending litany of menial chores. One day she had a simple realization that changed her life. That day she began to use her "chore time" as a time of prayer and fellowship with God.

Whenever Elizabeth walked the aisle of the supermarket, she prayed for each person who would eat the item of food she selected. On her way to pick up her children, she would lay their lives out before God, asking him to be there for them even when she couldn't. Each errand became an opportunity for fellowship with God. The chore that had been so tedious became a precious part of her routine that she cherished.

The purpose of these study guides is to help you use spiritual practices to make your own life richer, fuller, and deeper. The series includes twenty-four spiritual practices that are the building blocks of Christian spiritual formation. Each practice is a "holy habit" that has been modeled for us in the Bible. The practices are acceptance, Bible study and meditation, celebration, community, confession, contemplation, faith, fasting, forgiveness, gratitude, hospitality, justice, mentoring, outreach, prayer, reconciliation, Sabbath and rest, service, silence, simplicity, solitude, stewardship, submission, and worship.

As you move through the practices that you select, remember Christ's promise in Matthew 11:28–30:

Come to me, all of you who are weary and carry heavy burdens. Take my yoke upon you. Let me teach you, because I am humble and gentle at heart, and you will find rest for your souls. For my yoke is easy to bear, and the burden I give you is light.

Introduction

to the Practice of Acceptance & Gratitude

Some spiritual practices are more difficult than others, and in this set of studies the practice of acceptance is probably—under most circumstances—harder for many of us than practicing gratitude. How does one accept living with the consequences of somebody else's bad behavior? Or losing a relationship or a job through no fault of your own? How does a wife or mother accept the senseless death of her husband or child? How does a single person who has sorely desired marriage and family for decades truly accept living alone?

The first four chapters in this study focus on acceptance and tackle questions like these. But be prepared—there are no easy answers. Being a follower of Christ is no guarantee of being spared heartache and pain. Jesus said to his followers, "I have told you all this so that you may have peace in me. Here on earth you will have many trials and sorrows. But take heart, because I have overcome the world" (John 16:33). Jesus also told his followers to take up their crosses and follow him. But he did not say, "Take up your cross and

I'll follow you." Jesus went ahead of us and cleared the way; he shows us how to navigate the hard times in this life and promises peace with him.

Gratitude seems like a far less daunting spiritual practice. G. K. Chesterton noted, "When we were children we were grateful to those who filled our stockings at Christmas time. Why are we not grateful to God for filling our stockings with legs?" Sometimes all that's needed to be grateful is to look around us and see what we take for granted.

At other times—when we look around and see only hurt, anger, depression, turmoil—giving thanks is much more difficult. In Kelli Trujillo's meditation "Gratitude in Suffering" in the *Everyday Matters Bible for Women*, she notes that Joni Eareckson Tada calls 1 Peter 2:21 the "rule of thumb for any Christian struggling to understand God's purpose in hardship." Peter wrote, "God called you to do good, even if it means suffering, just as Christ suffered for you. He is your example, and you must follow in his steps." Trujillo observes that "pain, if we let it, can lead us into deeper intimacy with Christ. Is there anything more deserving of our gratitude?"

As you prepare to study acceptance and gratitude, here are some things you can do to prepare your heart and mind in order to get the most out of these studies:

- Make a list of the things in your life that you are having the most trouble accepting or being grateful for.

- Confess to God that you are struggling with these issues. Remember that you can be totally honest with God; that is one of the privileges of being in authentic relationship with him.

- Ask him to use your time of study to speak to your heart in a way that will help you move toward acceptance and gratitude.

- Return to your list after you've completed the four studies on each topic. Note any new insights, shifts or changes in your approach to the items on the list that you have gained during your time of study.

Our generous God enables us to do things we never thought possible. James wrote in his epistle, "Dear brothers and sisters, when troubles come your way, consider it an opportunity for great joy. . . . If you need wisdom, ask our generous God, and he will give it to you" (James 1:2, 5a).

Acceptance

CHAPTER 1

Can't Get No Satisfaction

Fighting Discontent

"This is what the Lord . . . says: Look at what's
happening to you! . . . You eat but are not satisfied.
You drink but are still thirsty. You put on clothes but
cannot keep warm. Your wages disappear as though
you were putting them in pockets filled with holes!"

HAGGAI 1:5-6

For this study, read Haggai 1–2:5.

In "Fighting Discontent" in the *Everyday Matters Bible for
Women*, Carolyn Arends talks about the fact that discontent
is nothing new. It goes back to Old Testament times. In fact,
it goes back to the beginning of the Bible. If Lucifer had
been content with his position in heaven, he wouldn't have
rebelled. If Adam and Eve had been content, they wouldn't
have eaten of the fruit of the Tree of Knowledge of Good
and Evil. The Israelites were discontent with the manna that
God was giving them every day in the wilderness. And to
this day, at any given time there is usually something in each
of our lives that we're not content with.

In this week's Scripture study passage, we learn that the children of Israel have neglected the temple and allowed it to fall into ruin. At the same time, we learn in verses 5–6 that their appetites have grown to the point where they want more and more food, drink, and clothes. God even says that their wages disappear as if they were "putting them in pockets filled with holes."

Sound familiar? In 2013, the average credit card debt per U.S. household was nearly $16,000. Nearly 15 percent of families spent 40 percent or more of their income on credit card payments. We want bigger houses, new cars, more clothes. Some of this is necessary, but some of it isn't. How many e-mails do you get every single day from companies that want to sell you things with nothing more than the click of a mouse? New furniture? We'll deliver it to your door! Makeup and shoes? Why go to the store? You can have it tomorrow without leaving your house! No wonder we're not content!

Discontent isn't limited to material things. Many of us are discontent with our marriage, job, or relationship with a friend, child, or parent. How many people do you know who are not happy with their appearance? The list goes on.

In today's Scripture reading, God tells the Israelites that their life is, as Carolyn Arends says, "a treadmill of diminishing returns" because they have neglected the temple. He instructs them to rebuild his house, which is the first step toward reconciliation with him. The purpose of the temple was first and foremost to be a place where the children of Israel would meet and spend time with God. Unless we spend time with God—in prayer, studying his word, singing his praises—we are bound to experience an emptiness that triggers a bottomless appetite for more. When we always want more, it is nearly impossible to be satisfied with what we have. Blaise Pascal said, "There is a God-shaped vacuum in the human heart which only God, made known through Jesus Christ, can fill."

"Content makes poor men rich; discontent makes rich men poor." —Benjamin Franklin

> **As you study this chapter, think about your own life. What are you most discontent with? How can you handle that in a healthy way?**

1. Why do you think the first study on acceptance focuses on discontent? What do the two have to do with each other?

2. In the study's Scripture reading, God expresses his anger with the Israelites and tells them to rebuild the temple. In Haggai 2:5, what does God promise his people? Are we told that they were contrite over their behavior? Why do you think that is not addressed in the story? What do you think prompted God to make that promise?

3. What do you think the connection is between spending time in the temple and addressing discontent? In your own experience, what impact does spending time with God have on one's discontent? Does it have any impact on our feelings of wanting more?

4. Is there a connection in this passage between the temple in Jerusalem and our bodies, the temple of the Holy Spirit?

5. Exodus 16 tells the story of how God provided food for the children of Israel while they were in the wilderness. Read the chapter and then consider why God stopped sending quail and bread for them to eat. Are there any parallels in your own life?

6. What are the areas in your life where you "eat but are not satisfied" and "drink but are still thirsty"? How might you address them?

"We would worry less if we praised more. Thanksgiving is the enemy of discontent." —Harry Ironside

Points to Ponder

In *The Pursuit of Holiness*, Jerry Bridges says, "Materialism wars against our souls in a twofold manner. First it makes us discontent and envious of others. Second, it leads us to pamper and indulge our bodies so that we become soft and lazy."

- Think about ways in which you may be envious of others, making you feel discontent.

- Think about how your life might have become "soft and lazy." What can you do to change this?

Prayer

Father, thank you for the blessings have you have showered on me. Thank you for [list at least five things for which you are thankful]:

Please give me a grateful spirit for what I have. Help me to focus more on that than on what I don't have.

Add your prayer in your own words.

Amen.

Put It into Practice

Try this experiment. The next time you find yourself wishing your life would change, think of someone who could use your help. Do something to encourage them, whether it's sending them a card, taking them cookies, or just picking up the phone to see how they are. After you've done that, try to remember what you were unhappy about; chances are it won't seem as distressing.

Take-away Treasure

If we concentrate on what we don't have, we will never have enough. If we concentrate on what we do have, most of the time we'll see that we really do have enough.

*For I have learned how to be content with whatever I have.
I know how to live on almost nothing or with everything. I
have learned the secret of living in every situation, whether it
is with a full stomach or empty, with plenty or little. For I can
do everything through Christ, who gives me strength.
(Philippians 4:11–13)*

❦

It's a Decision

Lessons from Leah

There was no sparkle in Leah's eyes, but Rachel
had a beautiful figure and a lovely face.

GENESIS 29:17

For this study, read Genesis 29:1–24.

If Laban's daughter Rachel was Cinderella, then her older
sister Leah was the Ugly Duckling.

Jacob had fallen deeply in love with Rachel and offered to
work for Laban seven years for free in order to marry her.
Genesis 29:20 tells us that "his love for her was so strong that
it seemed to him but a few days." He must have adored her!

Then there was Leah. She was the plain, older sister. She
had probably already experienced some pain by the very
proximity of her little sister Rachel, who was not only beautiful but also feisty and full of verve. It was probably very
difficult to have a front-row seat to Jacob and Rachel's love.
One wonders how Leah felt when her father tricked Jacob
into marrying her instead of Rachel and then exacted seven

more years of labor from him. Chances are those seven years didn't pass as quickly for Jacob as the first ones. What must it feel like to be married to a man who doesn't love you, a man who would rather be married to your beautiful sister? As Liz Curtis Higgs says in her article on Leah in the *Everyday Matters Bible for Women*, Leah was "yoked to a man who didn't choose her, love her, or want her." What a hard pill to swallow.

Even after Leah gave birth to three sons, Jacob remained indifferent. When Leah gave birth to her fourth son, somehow her heart changed. We are told that after Judah's birth Leah said, "Now I will praise the Lord."

"What a woman!" Higgs exclaims. "Instead of blaming God for what she didn't have, Leah thanked God for what she *did* have. . . . Leah had many reasons to become bitter and angry. Instead she chose to see God's goodness and faithfulness in her life and to praise him for them."

"You can't stop the waves, but you can learn to surf." —Joseph Goldstein

As you study this chapter, think about what is unfair or difficult in your life and your response to it.

1. At the beginning of this story, we're told that "there was no sparkle" in Leah's eyes. Why do you think that might have been so? What do "sparkling eyes" in one's expression usually indicate? How do you think Leah felt about this?

2. In Liz Curtis Higgs's article on Leah in the *Everyday Matters Bible for Women,* she says: "Three times she'd turned to a weak man for love. This time [after Judah's birth] she turned to a strong God." Is there a lesson for us in that action? How do you think it relates to her decision to praise God? Is there a connection between accepting one's situation and praising him?

3. Both Jacob and Rachel were unkind to Leah, to say the least. She had done nothing to earn her situation except to be plain and the instrument of her father's deception. She lived with a husband who did not love her, even when she gave him six sons and a daughter. Take a few minutes and try to put yourself in her place. How do you think you would have felt over the course of the years? What do you think triggered her decision to praise the Lord (v. 35)?

4. In Genesis 30:22, we're told that "God remembered Rachel's plight and answered her prayers by enabling her to have children" and she gave birth to Joseph. How do you think Leah responded to her sister having a son? Have you ever had a setback after you've accepted something that was hard for you? Can you resolve to accept it again?

5. What is happening in your life that you are having a difficult time accepting? Do you believe that God is in control of the situation? How do you think he wants you to handle it?

6. Are there some things in our lives that we should not accept? What are some examples? How should we react to those things?

"Acceptance of one's life has nothing to do with resignation; it does not mean running away from the struggle. On the contrary, it means accepting it as it comes, with all the handicaps of heredity, of suffering, of psychological complexes and injustices." —Paul Tournier

Points to Ponder

- The biblical account of Rachel paints a picture of a woman who was beautiful, smart, graceful, athletic, and cherished. From your reading of the account, do you think Rachel was happy? Why or why not?

- Is there anything from the story of Leah and Rachel that might apply to your life?

Prayer

God, give me grace to accept with serenity
the things that cannot be changed,
Courage to change the things
which should be changed,
and the Wisdom to distinguish
the one from the other.
Living one day at a time,
Enjoying one moment at a time,
Accepting hardship as a pathway to peace,
Taking, as Jesus did,
This sinful world as it is,
Not as I would have it,
Trusting that You will make all things right,
If I surrender to Your will,
So that I may be reasonably happy in this life,
And supremely happy with You forever in the next.
    —Reinhold Niebuhr

Add your prayer in your own words.

Amen.

Put It into Practice

Is there someone in your life who seems to get the best of you at every turn? If so, each time you think about that relationship or situation, will you decide (as many times as it takes) to praise and worship God instead?

Take-away Treasure

Anita Diamant's extraordinary novel *The Red Tent* tells the story of Leah and Rachel from the point of view of Dinah, the youngest child of Leah and Jacob. While much of the story is from the author's imagination, it is biblically based and presents a tremendous portrait of what life was like for women during Old Testament times, as well as probing the relationship among Jacob and his wives. Consider reading the book either on your own or with the group.

CHAPTER 3

Who Do You Think You Are?

Lessons from Job

"Where were you when I laid the foundations of
the earth? Tell me, if you know so much. Who
determined its dimensions and stretched out the
surveying line? . . . Have you ever commanded the
morning to appear and caused the dawn to rise in
the east? . . . Where does the light come from? And
where does darkness go? . . . Have you visited the
storehouses of the snow or seen the storehouses of
hail? . . . Who laid out the path for the lightning?"

JOB 38:4-5, 12, 19, 22, 25B

For this study, read Job 38–42. If possible, read all of Job.

Job was minding his own business. He was leading an
upright life that was pleasing to God. In fact, God was
so pleased with Job that he pointed him out to Satan and
called him "the finest man in all the earth. He is blameless—
a man of complete integrity. He fears God and stays away
from evil" (Job 1:8).

You know the rest of the story. Satan dares God to sorely test Job and see if Job continues to bless God. In fact, Satan predicts to God that Job will "curse you to your face" (Job 1:11). God takes Satan up on the dare and then Job's troubles begin—and one is worse than the other. In fact, they are catastrophic, and Job loses everything he has: his family, possessions, and health.

At first, Job is accepting of whatever befalls him. But finally he reaches his breaking point. By chapter 30, Job says, "I cry to you, O God, but you don't answer. . . . You have become cruel toward me. . . . Let the Almighty answer me. Let my accuser write out the charges against me. . . . I would tell him exactly what I have done. I would come before him like a prince" (Job 30:20–21; 31:35, 37). Who could blame him?

If someone was reading Job's story for the first time, they'd probably expect that God would at last tell Job about Satan's dare and commend Job for his steadfast faith. But the Bible is full of surprises, and instead of showing Job sympathy for all he's gone through, God enters the scene in chapter 38.

In a devastating, magnificent manner, God challenges Job and puts him in his place.

In one of the most powerful, exquisite passages in the Bible, God lays out one miracle after another that he has done. "Who are you to question me?" is essentially what he asks.

In chapter 40, Job says, "I am nothing. . . . I have said too much already" (vv. 4–5). But God isn't finished. He goes on with his challenge. No explanations. No apologies. Finally, in chapter 42, Job says, "I take back everything I said, and I sit in dust and ashes to show my repentance" (v. 6).

"Faith is not believing without proof—it is trusting without reservation." —*William Sloane Coffin*

As you study this chapter, remember that there are many, many questions in life that God has chosen not to answer. Think about why that might be.

1. In Job 7:1–4, Job says, "Is not all human life a struggle? Our lives are like that of a hired hand, like a worker who longs for the shade, like a servant waiting to be paid. I, too, have been assigned months of futility, long and weary nights of misery. Lying in bed, I think, 'When will it be morning?' But the night drags on, and I toss till dawn." Have you ever felt as Job did in this passage? Does bearing the pain seem a bit easier when you realize that others across the centuries throughout the world have also suffered? Does your suffering help increase your compassion and empathy for others?

2. If you're going through a trial right now, remember your past difficulties. How is this time different from the others? Do you have a particular way of coping? Do you find yourself praying more, or less?

3. In Job 9:33–35, Job says of God, "If only there were a mediator between us, someone who could bring us together. The mediator could make God stop beating me, and I would no longer live in terror of his punishment. Then I could speak to him without fear, but I cannot do that in my own strength." In Job 16:21, he says, "I need someone to mediate between God and me, as a person mediates between friends." Do you think Jesus is this longed-for "mediator"? If so, how does this make your relationship with God different from Job's? Compare the first passage about "terror" and "punishment" with the second one about "friends."

4. It takes Job a long time (at least forty chapters!) to accept what has happened to him. Notice that he does not ask for his family or riches to be restored. He simply humbles himself after God basically asks him, "Who do you think you are?" Have you reached moments like this when you have been able to accept what has happened to you? How did you feel once you did this—relieved, nervous, resigned?

5. Although Job's friends were no comforters to him during his suffering, he prayed for them after this knee-shaking confrontation with God. Scripture says that "when Job prayed for his friends, the Lord restored his fortunes. In fact, the Lord gave him twice as much as before!" (Job 42:10). What does this say to us about acceptance and moving on with no ill will toward others?

6. What does it really mean to say, as Job did, "The Lord gave me what I had, and the Lord has taken it away. Praise the name of Lord!" (Job 1:21)? Have you been able to do this when life seemed to go all wrong for you? How did this help you with accepting something difficult? Did it bring you any peace?

"Sometimes God doesn't tell us his plan because we wouldn't believe it anyway." —Carlton Pearson

Points to Ponder

• While this study doesn't cover Job's three friends, we know they were not particularly helpful to him. Do you have any friends like that? Have *you* ever been guilty of being one of Job's so-called comforters?

- Job discovered new depths to his faith as a result of his questioning. He was not afraid to speak out to God. While God's response was not what one might expect, it also was not the end of the story. Despite Job's questioning, God did not in the end withhold his blessings. In fact, he gave Job more than he initially had. Do you feel free to speak out to God and be totally honest with him?

Prayer

Father God, I have so many questions; there are so many things I do not understand. And often it seems like there are no answers, even from you. You have promised your children a peace that passes understanding. I pray for that peace even though I don't understand.

Forgive me for forgetting that it is you who laid the foundations of the earth; that you are the one who commands the sun to rise and set; that you know where the darkness goes.

Add your prayer in your own words.

Amen.

Put It into Practice

Is there something in your life that is completely outside your control? If so, commit it to God and trust in him, remembering that your Heavenly Father does indeed love you. Whatever trials you are going through may not make sense at this moment, but remember that "what we suffer now is nothing compared to the glory he will reveal to us later" (Romans 8:18).

Take-away Treasure

"I never imagined that my tough experiences would give me the substance I now need to minister to others. . . . Purposeful living is about hope. If you can hang onto the hope that God does have a plan for your life, as the Bible promises in Jeremiah 29:11, you'll make it through the tough days of the unknown, and later, the tough days of fulfilling the bold purposes God assigns you."—Katie Brazelton, "Purposeful Living in the Midst of Pain," *Everyday Matters Bible for Women*.

CHAPTER 4

When God Says No

Lessons from Gethsemane

> Then Jesus . . . prayed, "My Father! If this cup cannot
> be taken away unless I drink it, your will be done."
>
> MATTHEW 26:42

For this study, read Hebrews 12:1–4 and Matthew 26:36–46.

In "Lessons from the Cross," Jane Rubietta's excellent article
in the *Everyday Matters Bible for Women*, she makes an
extraordinary point we often overlook: The cross became a
"meeting place of relinquishment, relief, and relationship. . . .
[Jesus] gave up heaven to come to earth; he gave up earth to
take us to heaven."

The accounts of Jesus' time of prayer in the garden of Gethsemane present a very different picture from others that are
recorded. In Matthew's account, Jesus "became anguished
and distressed" (Matthew 26:37) and asked the disciples to
wait there for him while he prayed. Then we are told that
he "bowed with his face to the ground" (v. 39) as he asked
God to take away the cup of suffering that awaited him.

Then he added, "Yet I want your will to be done, not mine" (v. 39), and prayed again. Luke's account (22:39–46) adds three things: after Jesus' first prayer, an angel from heaven appeared and strengthened him; Jesus prayed even more fervently the second time; and finally, he was in "such agony of spirit that his sweat fell to the ground like great drops of blood" (v. 44).

When we think of the crucifixion story, it's easy to overlook the fact that Jesus *really didn't* want to be tortured and crucified. He was a man, but he was also the Son of God. One might think that with his power to perform miracles, maybe crucifixion wasn't as excruciating for him as it would be for a regular human being. But that wasn't true. There was only one way for Jesus to make his peace with what he was to endure, and that was to relinquish his will and accept the Father's.

We are not told whether or not Jesus thought it might be possible that God would hear his prayer and grant his petition, but it stands to reason that if Jesus didn't think there was a possibility of it, he wouldn't have spent himself to the point where he was sweating blood as he prayed.

The Father said no to Jesus and then watched his Son's agony. Jesus prayed so hard that an angel had to come to give him strength to pray more. The Father said no to his perfect Son. God said no to the Second Person of the Trinity. And Jesus accepted it.

"There are situations where I need to show more courage. . . . I have to ask myself, Is this what God wants me to do? And take the harder route."
—Carolyn Custis James, "Stretched in Scary Ways?" Everyday Matters Bible for Women

As you study this chapter, think about the times you've felt that God said no to you and how you responded.

1. Have you ever been in your own garden of Gethsemane? Are you there now? Perhaps you are single and have always wanted to marry. Maybe you want children but haven't been able to get pregnant. Or a loved one wasn't healed and died too young.

2. In Matthew 6:9–13, Jesus told us to "pray like this": "May your will be done on earth, as it is in heaven." Can you honestly pray for God's will to be done in your life and then entrust your situation to him?

3. What if his answer is not what you hoped for or expected? Think back on a time when this happened. How did it all work out? Better than you could have thought possible?

4. In the story of the patriarch Joseph, after he was sold by his angry brothers into slavery, Scripture records, "Meanwhile, the Midianite traders arrived in Egypt, where they sold Joseph to Potiphar" (Genesis 37:36). This was a dire situation for Joseph, but all along he trusted in his God. As we know, Joseph's placement in Potiphar's household eventually elevated him to the right hand of Pharaoh (although he had some hard years in prison before that could happen), and ultimately enabled him to help his own family. Have there been any "meanwhile" times in your life? Maybe now? Think back to how God did work out a situation in your life, despite the fact that you—like Joseph—felt abandoned for that season.

5. In Marilynne Robinson's Pulitzer Prize-winning novel
Gilead, her main character, Reverend John Ames, says:
"I have two choices: 1) To torment myself or 2) To trust the
Lord." Are you tormenting yourself over a situation right
now? If so, how can you give this over to God and then let
him act—whatever the answer?

6. What have you learned about trusting God no matter what?
If he says no to you regarding one door, he'll surely open another. As Kay Warren writes in the *Everyday Matters Bible for
Women*, "Whatever stage you're in, trust God with this season
of your life; accept its limits, but also relish its joys."

"What I'd have settled for
You've blown so far away
What You brought me to
I thought I could not reach
And I came so close to giving up
But You never did give up on me."
—*Rich Mullins, "Home,"* Winds of Heaven, Stuff of Earth

Points to Ponder

In his poem "Obedience," George MacDonald describes a conversation about following God's will, no matter how much it seems to go against our own:

> *I said, "Let me walk in the fields."*
>   *He said, "No, walk in the town."*
> *I said, "There are no flowers there."*
>   *He said, "No flowers, but a crown."* . . .
>
> *I pleaded for time to be given.*
>   *He said, "Is it hard to decide?*
> *It will not seem so in heaven*
>   *To have followed the footsteps of your Guide."*
>
> *I cast one look at the fields,*
>   *Then set my face to the town;*
> *He said, "My child, do you yield?*
>   *Will you leave the flowers for the crown?"*
>
> *Then into His hand went mine,*
>   *And into my heart came He;*
> *And I walk in a light divine*
>   *That path I had feared to see.*

• Have you ever had a conversation like this with God?

• Were you able to accept his will rather than your own?

Prayer

Father, as Jesus taught us to pray, your will be done as it is in heaven. Help me to know that your will is perfect. May I continually look to follow in the way you would have me go, and not in the way I think might be best or easiest for me.

Add your prayer in your own words.

Amen.

Put It into Practice

Think about the times when God has said no to your request, taking you instead in a different and better direction. Ask God to show you if there is anything in your life now where this may be true, and then ask him to give you the grace to accept whatever it may be. You may find, like MacDonald's obedient person, that you end up walking in a "light divine" down "that path [you] had feared to see"!

Take-Away Treasure

"Three different times I begged the Lord to take it away. Each time he said, 'My grace is all you need. My power works best in weakness.' So now I am glad to boast about my weaknesses, so that the power of Christ can work through me. . . . For when I am weak, then I am strong." (2 Corinthians 12:8–10)

"What's freeing is that it's not our light we're shining. When we come into relationship with Jesus, his light comes into us. And God's light will shine out of us—even through the cracks in our humanity—to provide a source of hope and light for those around us."—Elisa Morgan, "More Influence than You Realize," *Everyday Matters Bible for Women*

Notes / Prayer Requests

_____

_____

_____

_____

_____

_____

_____

_____

_____

_____

_____

_____

_____

_____

_____

_____

_____

_____

_____

_____

_____

_____

_____

Notes / Prayer Requests

Gratitude

CHAPTER 1

"It Would Have Been Enough"

Remembering God's Faithfulness

Give thanks to the Lord, for he is good!
His faithful love endures forever.

PSALM 136:1

For this study, read Psalm 136.

Celebrating Israel's return from exile in Babylon, Psalm 136 was written for use during worship in Jerusalem's rebuilt temple. Every year since then, even to the present, it has been a portion of the Passover service celebrated in Jewish synagogues and households all over the world. In many ways, this psalm is a short history of the extraordinary gifts and miracles God bestowed on the children of Israel over the course of their history, from sparing their firstborn in Egypt, to leading them to freedom over dry land across the Red Sea, to their arrival in the Promised Land. After the first line of each verse is read, the congregation responds with, "His faithful love endures forever."

During this part of the Passover service, right after Psalm 136 is recited, celebrants sing a song of remembrance and gratitude called *Dayenu*, a Hebrew word that translates as "it would have been enough." Had God brought the Jews out of Egypt, "it would have been enough." Had God split the Red Sea for them, "it would have been enough." Had he led them through dry land, "it would have been enough." Had he drowned their oppressors, "it would have been enough." The song enumerates fifteen instances of God's acts on their behalf, each one followed by singing *Dayenu*. The final stanza of the song says that any one of these gifts would have been enough, but God chose to do *all* of these things for his children. Here is the text of the last paragraph of the *Dayenu* section of the service:

> *Thus how much more so should we be grateful to the Omni-present One for the doubled and redoubled goodness that He has bestowed upon us; for He has brought us out of Egypt, and carried out judgments against them, and against their idols, and smote their first-born, and gave us their wealth, and split the sea for us, and took us through it on dry land, and drowned our oppressors in it, and supplied our needs in the desert for forty years, and fed us the manna, and gave us the Shabbat, and brought us before Mount Sinai, and gave us the Torah, and brought us into the land of Israel and built for us the Beit Habechirah to atone for all our sins.*

His faithful love endures forever.

"Let gratitude be the pillow upon which you kneel to say your nightly prayer. And let faith be the bridge you build to overcome evil and welcome good." —Maya Angelou

As you study this chapter, think about how God has indeed blessed you—not just recently, but over the course of the years.

1. Why is it important to recall God's past blessings in our lives as well as his current ones? During difficult times or in the midst of crises, what is the value of looking back to times of God's special blessing? How does this help move you forward during these crises?

2. The Old Testament records several instances in which a memorial object was chosen to remain as a reminder of God's faithfulness, ranging from Jacob's memorial pillar (Genesis 28:10–22), to a container of manna to be preserved for later generations (Exodus 16:32), to twelve memorial stones from the Jordan crossing (Joshua 1–9). Are there episodes in your life that are your own memorials to God's faithfulness?

3. Are there episodes in your life that are fitting subjects for your own version of *Dayenu*? What has God done for you that "would have been enough"?

4. In "Gratitude Driven by Love" in the *Everyday Matters Bible for Women*, Timothy Peck and JoHannah Reardon write of Psalm 136, "The refrain, 'His faithful love endures forever,' forms the basis for this command to thank God. The Hebrew word for *love* here is *hesed*, often translated as *steadfast love,* or covenant love. God's steadfast love is forever; it's not temporary or conditional." How has God displayed his steadfast love toward you? Think over your life and praise him for all he has done—whether it be strength to endure the hard times or joy for the good ones.

5. They also write, "The person convinced of the loyal love of God has a heart that naturally overflows with gratitude." Are you such a person? Are you convinced that God does indeed love you? If not, pray that he would help you to believe this. Read more psalms of thanksgiving or stories in the Bible where God has clearly worked in someone's life. Ask others in your group how they have seen God's love for them displayed in their lives.

6. In Revelation 4, John describes the worship that takes place in heaven. Read the chapter, focusing especially on verses 6–11. Why do you think the elders "fall down and worship the one sitting on the throne" (vv. 9–10) following the thanksgiving of others?

My heart is confident in you, O God; no wonder I can sing your praises with all my heart! . . . I will thank you, Lord, among all the people. I will sing your praises among the nations. For your unfailing love is higher than the heavens. Your faithfulness reaches to the clouds. (Psalm 108:1, 3–4)

Points to Ponder

- How has God moved in your life in a particular way? Is there something tangible that reminds you of this blessing?

- If you don't have one already, construct your own memorial pillar and then bring it to your group study next week and explain its significance. Afterward, keep it in a place where you can use it as your own remembrance.

- In "The Struggle to be Grateful" in the *Everyday Matters Bible for Women*, Mollie Ziegler Hemingway writes, "The truth is that we have so many things to be thankful for, including family, home, work, play, food, drink, and everything else that goes into daily life. But the God who provides these things has given us an even better gift: himself. . . . So rejoice and receive the gifts of God, confessing him and his goodness. Or as the psalmist says, 'Give thanks to the Lord, for he is good! His faithful love endures forever.'"

Prayer

Dear Lord, as I kneel upon the pillow of thanks, open my mind to remember your faithfulness; open my eyes to behold your gracious hand on my life; open my ears to hear the whispers of angels. Let my life be a song of praise.

Add your prayer in your own words.

Amen.

Put It into Practice

Do you ever talk to yourself? When you are walking in a circle trying to remember what you had been looking for, do you say to yourself, *Now what was I looking for?* Talking to ourselves can be a helpful tool in jogging the memory (as long as it is not a nonstop soliloquy!). In the same way, it is good for your mind and soul to tell you to praise the Lord. Even King David had to remind himself of it. Train your mind to remember regularly to tell yourself to praise the Lord. Beyond that, remind yourself, as David did, to do so with your whole heart. Doing so will help you remember the small things you've misplaced and also the great and wondrous good things God has shown and given you.

Take-away Treasure

Are you familiar with the ACTS prayer? While there is no right or wrong way to communicate with God, this format of prayer is recommended by many, including the Billy Graham Evangelistic Association. Here is how it works.

Organize your prayer in the following sequence: Adoration, Confession, Thanksgiving, and Supplication. There are many advantages to using this formula. First, we worship God; after all, that is why he created us. Next we confess our sins, not because God wants us to grovel, but because we are made in such a way that until we do confess, we are burdened by guilt. Now we thank God for everything: his creation, his love, his protection, all the gifts and blessings he showers down on us—even the ones we don't know about. The more specific we are about the things we thank

God for, the more we realize how very much God has given us. Finally, we make our petitions known to him. After we have done the previous three, our requests or supplications are likely to be in a more appropriate perspective.

If you use this format, share your experience of it with the group. If it is new to you, try it and report your responses back to the group.

CHAPTER 2

It Mattered to Jesus

The Value of Gratitude

Jesus asked, "Didn't I heal ten men? Where
are the other nine? Has no one returned to
give glory to God except this foreigner?"

LUKE 17:17–18

For this study, read Luke 17:11–19.

On his way to Jerusalem, Jesus encountered ten lepers who
cried out to him, "Jesus, Master, have mercy on us!" Schol-
ars tell us that nine of these men were Jewish and one was a
Samaritan. There was no love lost between the Jews and the
Samaritans—the Jews despised them, viewing them as un-
clean, uncivilized foreigners. But Jesus healed all ten men,
sending them to a priest, according to the Law of Moses
(see Leviticus 14:1–2).

Now that they were healed, the men could go back to their
homes and families; they could resume their work and rejoin
their communities. Jesus had given them their lives back.

We don't know where the other nine went following their healing, but we are told that the Samaritan came back to Jesus, fell down before him, and thanked him for the miraculous gift he had just bestowed on him. Jesus had two responses. First, he asked, "Where are the other nine?" You can almost hear his surprise and indignation that only one person came back to praise God and to say thank you. Second, Jesus told the Samaritan, "Stand up and go. Your faith has healed you."

We know Jesus didn't need to "feel good about himself" because the Samaritan showed his gratitude. In fact, there are many instances in the Gospels where Jesus told people not to tell others of the blessings and miracles he had bestowed on them. So what was it about the man's return that moved Jesus? Perhaps it was because Jesus knew that gratitude is not solely for the benefit of the giver but of equal—maybe even more—benefit to the recipient. Perhaps it is simply enough to know that when we have an "attitude of gratitude," it is pleasing to the Lord.

"The words 'thank you' are probably the greatest words in any language." —Mister (Fred) Rogers

As you study this chapter, think about why you give thanks, both to God and to other people. Think about how you feel if you neglect to do that. And consider how you think God responds when you come back to him and say, "Thank you."

1. Why do you think Jesus was surprised and displeased that the other lepers didn't come back? Did he heal them in order for them to be grateful? Why do you think Jesus thought it was important for all ten to return and say thank you? Why do we expect others to thank us when we do a good deed for them?

2. Jesus said to the Samaritan, "Your faith has healed you." Do you think he was solely talking about the leper's physical healing?

3. Jesus looked at the lepers and told them to "go show yourselves to the priests." Then, as they went, "they were cleansed of their leprosy." Does this suggest that even a look by Jesus could bring about healing? How might this kind of healing show itself today?

4. Interestingly, Jesus did not go to the lepers, nor did he have them approach him. He simply gave them instructions from a distance about what to do. What do you make of this? He certainly wasn't afraid to touch lepers, which he had done in other circumstances (Matthew 8:3). Why might Jesus have handled this occasion from a distance? Have you ever neglected to thank someone who helped you whose help was from afar? Does inconvenience justify negligence?

5. Only one, when he saw that he was healed, came back to Jesus, shouting, "Praise God!" He fell face down on the ground at Jesus' feet, thanking him. What does the gesture of falling face down signal in this moment of gratitude? Have you ever felt such thanks that you, too, wanted to prostrate yourself before the giver?

6. What have you forgotten to give thanks for? Is it ever too late to do so?

*Be filled with the Holy Spirit, singing psalms and
hymns and spiritual songs among yourselves, and
making music in your hearts. And give thanks
for everything to God the Father in the name of
our Lord Jesus Christ. (Ephesians 5:18–20)*

Points to Ponder

Harry Genet tells the story of German pastor Martin
Rinkart, who served in the walled town of Eilenburg during
the horrors of the Thirty Years War of 1618–1648. Eilenburg became an overcrowded refuge for the surrounding
area, and the fugitives suffered from epidemic and famine.
At the beginning of 1637, the year of the Great Pestilence,
there were four ministers in Eilenburg. But one abandoned
his post for healthier areas and could not be persuaded
to return. Pastor Rinkhart officiated at the funerals of the
other two. As the only pastor left in the town, Rinkhart
often conducted services for as many as forty to fifty people
a day—some 4,480 in all. In May of that year, his own wife
died. By the end of the year, the refugees had to be buried in
trenches without services. Yet living in a world dominated
by death, Pastor Rinkart wrote the following prayer for his
children to offer to the Lord:

Now thank we all our God
With hearts and hands and voices;
Who wondrous things hath done,
In whom this world rejoices
Who, from our mother's arms,
Hath led us on our way,
With countless gifts of love,
And still is ours today.

• Think of areas in your life where you might have difficulty being grateful.

• Pray about ways to trust God and to be thankful for all things. "If you can't be thankful for what you receive, be thankful for what you escape" (Anonymous).

Prayer

Lord, help me always to remember that your gifts are never-ending, both immediate and from afar. Please help me to be ever mindful of those gestures of grace that come from afar and are not always in my immediate range of vision.

Add your prayer in your own words.

Amen.

Put It into Practice

Always remember that the most important words in the human language are *thank you*. Keep a set of thank-you cards by your bedside. Pick a night each week to write one note to someone who gave you a blessing that week. If you don't have time to send a card, drop that person an e-mail—or better yet, express your gratitude when you next meet!

Take-away Treasure

Find a moment every day—especially during a stressful interlude—to breathe deeply and give thanks. You'll find a whole new set of coping skills!

CHAPTER 3

Thank God Anyway

Gratitude in the Midst of Uncertainty

"Oh, how my soul praises the Lord. How
my spirit rejoices in God my Savior!"

LUKE 1:46-47

For this study, read Luke 1:26–56.

We don't learn much about in the New Testament about
Jesus' mother Mary, particularly as a young girl. We are told
in Matthew 1:18–19 that Mary was engaged to Joseph when
she became pregnant. Joseph "did not want to disgrace her
publicly, so he decided to break the engagement quietly." In
today's reading in Luke, we learn about Gabriel's visit to her
announcing that she has found favor with God and that she
will give birth to the Son of the Most High.

Mary was a young teenager when all this happened. She
was barely more than a girl when Gabriel told her she
would soon bear a son conceived through the Holy Spirit.
What thoughts must have swirled through her mind as

she learned what was to come. Her whole future had been turned upside down in the space of just a few minutes.

A virgin birth had never occurred in the history of mankind. Perhaps Mary was chosen by God because she trusted him and gave thanks in all kinds of circumstances. But there must have been moments when she wondered about her future, suffered at the prospect of losing Joseph, wondered about the prospect of being rejected by others.

While we don't learn how her parents responded to the news, it's very possible they were distressed and embarrassed by their young daughter's pregnancy out of wedlock. We don't even know whether they believed Mary's account of Gabriel's visit. Joseph was planning to break the engagement, albeit discreetly, so his initial response had to be one of disappointment and upset.

Just a few days after she received Gabriel's news, Mary visited Elizabeth, who would soon give birth to John the Baptist. It is there that Mary offered a song of praise to the Lord (Luke 1:46–56): "Oh, how my soul praises the Lord. How my spirit rejoices in God my Savior!" From the moment she learned that God had appointed her for this extraordinary experience, Mary's life was full of uncertainty. But she thanked God anyway.

The shepherd boy with just five small stones and a slingshot didn't know whether his meager weapon would bring down the giant Goliath (1 Samuel 17:1–50). The immediate future must have looked pretty bleak to Shadrach, Meshach, and Abednego when Nebuchadnezzar had them thrown into a blazing furnace (Daniel 3:19–30). The poor widow who visited Elisha could hardly have imagined that her small flask of oil would multiply and meet her mammoth needs (2 Kings 4:1–7). Then there were Ruth, Esther, and Daniel. They were all in the jaws of uncertainty; yet like Mary, they thanked God in advance. They thanked him anyway.

"God is in control, and therefore in everything I can give thanks—not because of the situation but because of the One who directs and rules over it." —Kay Arthur

As you study this chapter, think about areas in your life where God might want you to thank him anyway.

1. We tend to think of gratitude as saying thank you after the fact. What does saying thank you before the fact look like?

2. The biblical accounts of Daniel, Shadrach and his two friends, along with Ruth, Esther, and many others like them, do not necessarily tell us that they thanked God in the midst of their uncertainty. Why can we be certain that they did? Is gratitude always only evidenced by the words "thank you"?

3. Put yourself in Joseph's place when he learned of Mary's pregnancy, and in the place of her parents when they heard that they were about to become grandparents. How would you have responded? What are some ways that Mary may have suffered for the privilege of bearing the Son of God that are not revealed in the Gospel accounts?

4. Read the Magnificat, Mary's song of praise in Luke 1:46–55. Verse 49 says, "For the Mighty One is holy, and he has done great things for me." Do you think you would have felt that if you were an unmarried pregnant teenage girl, especially in her culture when such people were stoned for breaking the Law of Moses?

5. Luke 1:5–25 tells the story of Elizabeth and Zechariah. When Gabriel announced the impending birth of a son, Zechariah's reaction was very different from Mary's. How did he respond? Why do you think that Gabriel imposed the punishment of making Zechariah unable to speak?

6. Read Luke 1:57–66. We learn that as soon as Zechariah wrote after his son's birth, "His name is John," then Zechariah's ability to speak returned. Why do you think it returned at that particular time? What did Zechariah do as soon as he could speak again? What significance do you think these two actions have? Are there ways this story applies to your own life?

"The optimist says, the cup is half full. The pessimist says, the cup is half empty. The child of God says, my cup runneth over." —Anonymous

Points to Ponder

- One way of defining faith is saying thank you anyway. What are the "anyways" in your life?

- "Anyway" is simply a combination of the words *any* and *way*. Are you willing to thank God for any way he allows your life to proceed?

Prayer

Father of all mercies, I confess to you that I have worried about my future, that my faith works better in reverse than in advance. I thank you for the gifts and wonders you have already worked on my behalf. Thank you for those that lie ahead. I ask for your sustenance, strength, and peace when I fret over things that may lie ahead.

Add your prayer in your own words.

Amen.

Put It into Practice

This week, choose a fear or uncertainty that is troubling you. Each time you think of it, breathe a prayer of thanks to God. Remember, like the man who came to Jesus for healing for his son in Mark 9:24, you can always say, "I do believe, but help me overcome my unbelief."

Take-away Treasure

When you are feeling fear or worry, anxiety or concern, use the secret weapon of song. Sing or listen to songs such as "It Is Well with My Soul" or "You Are My Hiding Place," or any song of praise and worship. You'll be surprised by the results!

CHAPTER 4

We Bless Your Name

Gratitude in the Midst of Suffering

> So the jailer put them into the inner dungeon and
> clamped their feet in stocks. Around midnight
> Paul and Silas were praying and singing hymns
> to God and the other prisoners were listening.
>
> ACTS 16:24-25

For this study, read Acts 16:16–40.

What's worse than being in prison? Possibly being in prison when you're innocent of any wrongdoing. That was the situation for Paul and Silas when they were in Philippi. They had expelled a demon from a fortune-teller who had been following them through the city shouting, "These men are servants of the Most High God, and they have come to tell you how to be saved." The fortune-teller had earned a lot of money for her masters, who were furious to have lost such a good source of income. They "grabbed Paul and Silas and dragged them before the authorities" (v. 19), complaining that they were causing an uproar. The city officials ordered that they be stripped, severely beaten with wooden rods, and then thrown into a prison dungeon with their feet clamped in stocks.

They must have been in that cold, damp, dark prison for many hours. Bleeding, hurting, aching, unclothed, and uncertain of what would happen next, Paul and Silas chose to pray and sing hymns, and they must have been loud because the other prisoners listened to their songs and petitions. It's one thing to be grateful to God when things are going well; it's quite another to thank and praise him when things are going badly. And things were going very badly for Paul and Silas.

Then the impossible happened: an earthquake shook so violently that the prison doors flew open and every prisoner's chains were loosed. But Paul and Silas didn't flee. In fact, they must have convinced the other prisoners to stay where they were, because they reassured the jailer that no one had left. The jailer was so astounded that he and his family became believers.

Joni Eareckson Tada was shackled in the chains of paralysis at the tender age of sixteen; her body became her prison. In his providence, God has allowed Joni to remain paralyzed in the decades that have ensued, and she has spoken of the deep pain and despair she has experienced at times. During an interview, Joni was asked what she will say to God when she meets him in heaven. She answered that the first thing she will do—despite her longing to walk and run and dance—will be to remain paralyzed for just a minute longer in order to offer God one extra "moment of paralyzed praise." She will choose to remain in prison a little longer than she must, just like Paul and Silas.

"God had one son on earth without sin, but never one without suffering." —St. Augustine

As you study this chapter, think about the things that may be imprisoning you now. How can today's study help you in the midst of your suffering?

1. Why do you think that Paul and Silas remained in jail after their chains were loosed? Have you ever chosen to stay in a place that you wanted desperately to leave for a larger purpose?

2. Why do you think the other prisoners stayed in prison even though their chains had fallen off and they could have left?

3. The fortune-teller was actually proclaiming that Paul and Silas were men of God who were offering the way of salvation. Why do you think they silenced her?

4. What is the value of singing praises to God as well as worshipping him in prayer?

5. What is the value of suffering?

6. What do you think Joni Eareckson means by "paralyzed praise"? Do you have your own version of that to offer God? Why might he want that?

"We were promised sufferings. They were part of the program. We were even told, 'Blessed are they that mourn.'" —C. S. Lewis

Points to Ponder

"Contrary to what might be expected, I look back on experiences that at the time seemed especially desolating and painful, with particular satisfaction. Indeed, I can say with complete truthfulness that everything I have learned in my seventy-five years in this world, everything that has truly enhanced and enlightened my existence, has been through affliction and not through happiness, whether pursued or attained. In other words, if it ever were to be possible to eliminate affliction from our earthly existence by means of some drug or other medical mumbo jumbo . . . the result would not be to make life delectable, but to make it too banal or trivial to be endurable. This of course is what the cross signifies, and it is the cross more than anything else, that has called me inexorably to Christ."

—Malcolm Muggeridge

- Think about how Malcolm Muggeridge's words may be true in your life.

- John Wesley said, "The readiest way to escape from our sufferings is to be willing that they should endure as long as God pleases." What do you think he meant?

Prayer

Our Father, who is in heaven, you have promised your
children that when we join you in heaven, there will be
no more suffering. But here on earth there is plenty.
When I am suffering, please remind me to thank you for
your many mercies and blessings; please remind me to
sing songs of praise and worship. Help me to hope for
relief but to rely on you for whatever comes next.

Add your prayer in your own words.

Amen.

Put It into Practice

Is there something shackling you today that you can offer to
God as your own form of paralyzed praise?

Take-Away Treasure

In his book *Walking with God through Pain and Suffering,*
Timothy Keller says, "You don't really know Jesus is all you
need until Jesus is all you have." If you are feeling stripped of
the things you need, remember who you have.

Notes / Prayer Requests

Notes / Prayer Requests

_____

_____

_____

_____

_____

_____

_____

_____

_____

_____

_____

_____

_____

_____

_____

_____

_____

_____

_____

Leader's Guide

to Acceptance & Gratitude

Thoughts on Where to Meet

- If you have the chance, encourage each group member to host a gathering. But make sure your host knows that you don't expect fresh baked scones from scratch or white-glove-test-worthy surroundings. Set the tone for a relaxed and open atmosphere with a warm welcome wherever you can meet. The host can provide the space and the guests can provide the goodies.

- If you can't meet in homes, consider taking at least one of your meetings on the road. Can you meet at a local place where people from your community gather? A park or a coffee shop or other public space perhaps.

- If you meet in a church space, consider partnering with another local church group and take turns hosting. How can you extend your welcome outside your group?

Thoughts on Ways to Foster Welcome

- If many of your members have a hard time meeting due to circumstances, look for ways to work around it. Consider providing childcare if there are moms who have difficulty attending, or meet in an accessible space if someone who might want to join has a disability. Does a morning time work better? Could you meet as smaller groups and then get together as a larger group for an event? Be flexible and see how you can accommodate the needs of the group. Incorporate "get to know you" activities to promote sharing. Don't take yourselves too seriously and let your humor shine through.

Incorporating Other Practices

- *Lift your voices.* Integrate worship throughout the study. Find songs that speak about acceptance and gratitude.

- *Commit to lift each other up in prayer.* You may want to have a prayer walk as part of seeing opportunities to serve in your community, or prayer partners who might be able to meet at other times.

- *Dig deep into the word.* Take the study at your own pace but consider including passages for participants to read in between meetings. The *Everyday Matters Bible for Women* has a wealth of additional resources.

- *Celebrate!* Bring cupcakes and candles, balloons or anything celebratory to distribute to each member of the group. Ask each person to share something that they want to celebrate today, be it an event, a new insight, or anything they choose.

Acceptance

The spiritual practice of acceptance is one of the most challenging of all the spiritual disciplines. Accepting things that simply seem unacceptable goes against every fiber of our beings.

Chapter 1: Some members of the group might find it surprising that a study on acceptance would begin with a chapter on discontent. If you feel it's appropriate for your group, start the discussion by asking if anyone had that reaction. Let the group discuss the connections between discontent and acceptance. In the Old Testament, there are many stories of discontent—it seems that the children of Israel were always murmuring or complaining about something. Point out some of the stories covered in chapter 1 and ask the group to think of others. How did God respond to those complaints? Were any of their complaints justified?

You might also want to focus on the connection that Scripture makes between God's response to the people's discontent and his instruction to rebuild the temple. Is there a connection? Is there an insight that is pertinent to the group?

Chapter 2: The story of Leah and Rachel is as interesting in its treatment of Laban and Jacob as it is of the two women. In her article, Liz Curtis Higgs calls Jacob "a weak man." What does the group think she meant by that? Discuss what else we know about Jacob; for example, his complicity with his mother Rebecca in wresting Esau's birthright or his partiality for his youngest son Joseph in later years. Was he a good son? Brother? Father? Laban seems like a duplicitous, scheming liar, yet we are never told of him "paying for his sins." Who comes off best in this story? Is there a lesson for us today in the story?

Chapter 3: The story of Job could easily require more than one session for the group to discuss so many issues. The obvious question here is, "Why me?" But ask the group, in Job's experience or their own, to think about the question, "Why not me?" How are we to make our peace when God simply does not tell us why terrible, undeserved things happen? Did God have any advice to Job about how to do that? While God did restore Job's good fortune, Job is a changed man and his situation is also changed. How has he changed because of the events that took place? Job was given a new set of children, but we know that children are not interchangeable. Why do you think God allowed his original children to die? How have the members of your group changed as a result of tragedy in their lives? Are the changes all bad? Are there any results that have been valuable to them? Feel free to extend this study to two weeks if you think the group wants to discuss this issue further.

Chapter 4: "When God Says No" is probably the most difficult issue of all to confront in this group of studies. While he has said no in many other biblical accounts, the account in this chapter is the most telling. Why? Because God the Father said no to his own Son. God said no to something that was not fair in order to provide something that also isn't fair: mercy to mankind for all ages. God said no to Jesus, but he simultaneously said no to Satan for eternity.

A 45-year-old woman, who had always wanted marriage and a family above any other thing in this life, was blessed by God with an extraordinary career, a number of deep friendships, and a life many would consider privileged. Except for one thing: what she wanted so much more was a life with a godly husband who would love her and children whom she could nurture and love. While she was grateful for the wonderful things that God *had* given her, she couldn't understand why he had not given her the desire of her heart. She prayed for a husband and family of her own for decades. One day after God had moved in an incredible way in her life, she realized that God is indeed interested in every single part of his children's lives, the "number of hairs on their heads." Then it dawned on her that God had turned down his own Son Jesus in the garden of Gethsemane. Her next thought was this: *If God could say no to his own son and that was good enough for Jesus, it had better be good enough for me.* If you think your group would benefit from this story, share it with them.

Gratitude

Chapter 1: In many ways, this chapter is about souvenirs. *Souvenir* is the French word meaning "to remember." We keep souvenirs of a special trip or event to remind us of how we felt at the time. *Dayenu* is a souvenir in the form of a song, a sort of symbolic "memorial pillar" that the Israelites designated as physical reminders of God's hand at a particular time and place in their history. In times of trouble or sorrow when it is especially difficult to be grateful, it helps to have a physical reminder of God's faithfulness at a specific point in one's life. It can serve as encouragement for the present and the future as well as a memory of the past. Ask the members of your group to think of a time when God was particularly faithful in their lives. Have them create their own "memorial pillars," and bring them to the next meeting and tell the stories behind their souvenirs.

Chapter 2: Jesus wasn't one of those sensitive sorts of thin-skinned people who take offense easily. In the Gospels, we see him expressing righteous anger; he doesn't hesitate to reprimand others or correct them in matters that count for the kingdom. But he doesn't go off and sulk because someone didn't stroke his ego. So this story of the one leper who came back to thank Jesus is unusual; in fact, it's the only one of its kind in all of the Gospel accounts of Jesus' life on earth. Why do you think he so valued the act of saying thank you?

When your group meets to discuss this chapter, give each of them two thank-you notes, one blank one and one you've written to her. In yours, be sure to express a specific quality she possesses or a gesture you appreciate. Then ask each member to use the blank note to write her own thank-you note to Jesus for his healing in her own life.

Chapter 3: Truth be told, if we're alive, then we're in the midst of uncertainty. Thanks be to God, he has given us the capacity to forget that most of the time. If we didn't, we'd never be able to do anything; we'd be paralyzed by fear of all the potential disasters around us! But when we *are* aware of the uncertainty surrounding us, which is usually when we are facing something new—or something we fear—that's when we worry.

This chapter is about the connection between gratitude and worry. That's where "thank God" meets "anyway." Yes, Mary could have been disowned by her family; she could have been stoned for getting pregnant out of wedlock; she could have said to Gabriel, "But what if . . . ?" when he told her his news. But Mary praised God. She said, "How my spirit rejoices in God my Savior! For he took notice of his lowly servant girl, and from now on all generations will call me blessed" (Luke 1:47–48). Instead of worrying, Mary said, "Thank you, God!" When your group meets, ask each member to name out loud something she is worried about and then say, "Thank you, God!"

Chapter 4: Before your group meets, try to secure a recording of Selah's song, "I Bless Your Name." The song recounts the story of Paul and Silas's prison experience. The last stanza is: "Some midnight hour, if you should find you're in a prison in your mind, reach out and praise. Defy those chains, and they will fall in Jesus' name." Have this song playing as the group enters or when you start the study. The prison of our mind is usually harsher and harder to bear than any physical cell. It often feels like a locked door with no key. At the end of your meeting, consider giving each member a key (blank keys at locksmith shops are very inexpensive) to remind her of the power of gratitude even in the midst of suffering.

EVERYDAY MATTERS BIBLE STUDIES
for women

Spiritual practices for everyday life

Acceptance	Mentoring
Bible Study & Meditation	Outreach
Celebration	Prayer
Community	Reconciliation
Confession	Sabbath & Rest
Contemplation	Service
Faith	Silence
Fasting	Simplicity
Forgiveness	Solitude
Gratitude	Stewardship
Hospitality	Submission
Justice	Worship

HENDRICKSON
PUBLISHERS

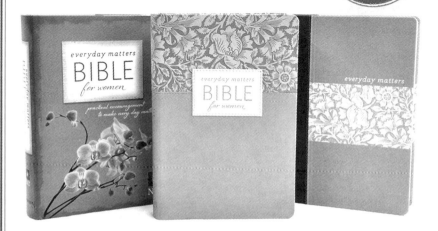